HENRY IV, PART 1: A GUIDE

The Shakespeare Handbooks

Available now:

- Antony & Cleopatra

- As You Like It

- Hamlet

- Henry IV, Part 1

- King Lear

- Macbeth

- A Midsummer Night's Dream

- Romeo & Juliet

- Twelfth Night

Further titles in preparation.

The Shakespeare Handbooks are available at bookshops, or direct from the publisher at www.shakespeare-handbooks.com.

The Shakespeare Handbooks

Henry IV
Part 1

A Guide

by Alistair McCallum

Upstart Crow Publications

First published in 2014 by
Upstart Crow Publications

Copyright © Alistair McCallum 2014

A CIP catalogue record for this book
is available from the British Library

ISBN 978 1 899747 05 4

Printed in the UK by Berforts Information Press Ltd,
23 – 25 Gunnels Wood Park, Gunnels Wood Road,
Stevenage, Herts SG1 2BH

Upstart Crow Publications is a division of
The Language Studio Ltd

www.shakespeare-handbooks.com

Setting the scene

Shakespeare wrote *King Henry IV, Part 1* in or around 1596. He was in his early thirties, a successful actor and dramatist, and a member – and shareholder – of the Lord Chamberlain's Men, the most prestigious theatre company in London.

English history was a topic of intense interest at the time, providing the subject-matter for nine of Shakespeare's plays during the 1590s. The defeat of the Spanish Armada in 1588 had kindled a powerful sense of national identity and unity; but hostilities continued for years to come, and England was also involved in expensive military adventures in Ireland, France and the Netherlands. At home, food shortages, unemployment and high inflation led to frequent social unrest: political disputes among the Queen's ministers added to the sense of instability. The Queen herself – in her sixties at the time the play was written – was unmarried and childless, and the question of who should succeed her was fraught with speculation and anxiety.

Against this background, plays that chronicled England in states of crisis were extremely popular. Through the medium of history they addressed issues central to the Tudor dynasty: for example, should the basis of monarchy be purely hereditary, or was it more important to select an effective ruler in the interests of stability and unity? Was it ever right to rebel against an unjust monarch – or to depose a weak one?

History plays of the time were generally limited to the actions of kings and noblemen, and often drew heavy-handed moral lessons. *King Henry IV*, by contrast, presented history in a more realistic, balanced way, involving a wide range of vividly-drawn characters from different classes – including the inimitable Falstaff. The play was an immediate success, both on the stage and in print; it was reprinted more frequently than any other play by Shakespeare during his lifetime. It has remained a favourite throughout the centuries.

"Henry IV, Part 1 was a highly innovative work in 1596 for precisely the reasons that make it one of the greatest of Shakespeare's history plays. It marks an advance both in Shakespeare's development and in the growth of English drama, for, by repeatedly shifting its focus between affairs of state and bawdy irreverence, the play presents a composite image of a whole society, something that had never been attempted before ... Groundbreaking in its own day, Henry IV, Part 1 is still impressive in ours, due to the range of people, events, and language, from the most casual ribaldry to the boldest rhetoric, realistically presented on stage."

Charles Boyce, *Shakespeare A to Z*, 1990

A heavy burden

A year has passed since the death of King Richard the Second.

His cousin, Henry Bolingbroke, taking advantage of the king's unpopularity, had executed Richard's prominent supporters, deposed Richard, and proclaimed himself King Henry the Fourth. One of the new king's followers, hoping for royal favour, had then murdered Richard.

The removal of Richard – who, if alive, could have become a figurehead for future rebellions – was clearly to King Henry's advantage. However, the new king, on seeing Richard's coffin, angrily denounced his murderer, promising to atone for his death with a pilgrimage to Jerusalem:

> *King:*   I'll make a voyage to the Holy Land,
> To wash this blood off from my guilty hand.
> March sadly after; grace my mournings here,
> In weeping after this untimely bier.

Henry has succeeded in becoming king; but the vigour of the younger Bolingbroke has been overshadowed by weariness and anxiety now that he has achieved his ambition. There are those who question the new king's authority, and rebellion is already brewing in a number of places within the kingdom.

To make matters worse, it is common knowledge that the king's eldest son Harry is spending his time with disreputable companions in taverns and brothels, and neglecting his duties as Prince of Wales.

Curtain up

No peace for the new king

King Henry is in council with his noblemen. The deposition of his predecessor, King Richard the Second, was accompanied by widespread bloodshed and turmoil, and the first year of his reign has not been easy.

> *King:* So shaken as we are, so wan with care,
> Find we a time for frighted peace to pant[1] ...
>
> [1] *catch its breath*

Civil conflict must never be allowed to afflict the country again, he declares:

> *King:* The edge of war, like an ill-sheathed knife,
> No more shall cut his master.

But warfare is still on the king's mind. England's military energies, he announces, are to be directed abroad, in the form of a Christian crusade to rid the Holy Lands of the infidels who now inhabit them.

However, the king's pledge to travel to Jerusalem is well known; it is now a year since the murder of King Richard, the event that prompted Henry to make his promise. He asks the Earl of Westmoreland what progress has been made in preparing for the expedition.

Westmoreland explains that a great deal of enthusiastic discussion and practical planning for the crusade has been taking place. However, preparations have been cut short by grave news from Wales, where the English are contending with a ferocious rebellion led by Owen Glendower. An English army led by Edmund Mortimer has been defeated and butchered, and Mortimer himself has been captured.

There may be further bad news, warns Westmoreland. A Scottish army, with the fearsome Earl of Douglas at its head, has invaded the north of England. English troops led by young Henry Percy, son of the Earl of Northumberland, have confronted the Scots at Holmedon. The result of the battle is not yet known, says Westmoreland.

Some critics have accused Shakespeare of propagating the 'Tudor myth' in his history plays. According to this version of history, the sacrilegious removal of the rightful king Richard II by Henry IV in 1399 led to divine punishment, in the form of decades of discord and civil strife, culminating in the carnage of the Wars of the Roses; and it was not until eighty years later, with the accession of the first Tudor monarch, Henry VII – grandfather of Elizabeth I – that peace and stability were restored.

While this view of history was encouraged by the Tudor establishment, it seems unlikely that Shakespeare accepted it unquestioningly.

"... Shakespeare approached his sources not as a spokesman of government orthodoxy but as a creative artist whose business was to explore, not expound; he invented characters and episodes which make that exploration more complex; the role of Providence in the plays is deeply ambiguous; he shows a sophisticated awareness of history as ironical, baffling, and frequently unfair."

Levi Fox, *The Shakespeare Handbook*, 1987

The king, however, has already been informed of the outcome by Sir Walter Blunt, who has ridden back from Holmedon with good news: Henry Percy has defeated Douglas, and many Scottish noblemen have been taken prisoner.

The king reflects sadly on the contrast between Percy (nicknamed 'Hotspur'), renowned for his courage and honour, and his own son, Prince Henry, heir to the throne, who is living a debauched and dishonourable life.

Whilst rejoicing at Percy's victory, the king is displeased with the young man's refusal to hand over his valuable prisoners to the king, as is customary. Hotspur has offered just one captive, a member of the Scottish royal family, to the king. Westmoreland warns him that this shows the influence of Hotspur's uncle – Thomas Percy, Earl of Worcester – who, he claims, is implacably hostile to the king.

The king replies that he has already sent for Henry Percy and will demand an explanation for his provocative action. He calls the council to a close, wishing to continue the discussion in private with Westmoreland, unwilling to say anything further in public in his state of displeasure.

> *King:*   … more is to be said and to be done
> Than out of anger can be uttered.

For the present, any plans for an expedition to Jerusalem must be set aside.

Bad company

I, ii

Prince Henry (also known as Harry or Hal) is spending time with Sir John Falstaff, one of his usual companions. Falstaff – in all likelihood suffering from over-indulgence in alcohol – asks Hal what time of day it is.

The prince teases the older man relentlessly. Why should a corrupt, obese, lazy drunkard like him need to know the time?

> *Prince:*   What a devil hast thou to do with the time of the day?
> Unless hours were cups of sack,[1] and minutes
> capons,[2] and clocks the tongues of bawds, and dials
> the signs of leaping-houses,[3] and the blessed sun
> himself a fair hot wench in flame-coloured taffeta,
> I see no reason why thou shouldst be so superfluous
> to demand the time of the day.

> [1] *heavy, rich white wine*
> [2] *chickens*
> [3] *brothels*

"Thirty-six big plays in five blank verse acts, and not a single hero! Only one man in them all who believes in life, enjoys life, thinks life worth living ... and that man – Falstaff!"

George Bernard Shaw, *Better than Shakespear?*, preface to *Three Plays for Puritans*, 1901

Falstaff replies that the day is indeed of little interest to him; as a thief, he is proud to be governed by the moon and stars. He appeals to Hal to be tolerant, when he inherits the throne, of thieves like himself:

> *Falstaff:*   Marry then sweet wag, when thou art king let not us that are squires of the night's body be called thieves of the day's beauty: let us be Diana's[1] foresters, gentlemen of the shade, minions of the moon …
>
> [1] *goddess of the moon and of hunting*

Hal agrees that Falstaff's fortunes, governed by the moon like the tides of the ocean, will fall and rise – from the foot of the ladder at the bottom of the gallows, for example, to the beam at the top. The two continue to banter about their favorite subjects: women, taverns, and the risks and rewards of crime.

Falstaff claims, unconvincingly, that the prince has been a bad influence on him, and declares his intention give up his life of crime. However, he agrees without hesitation to take part in a robbery planned for the next day.

At this point their acquaintance Ned Poins, a seasoned thief and Falstaff's regular accomplice, joins them. He outlines his plans for a highway robbery. The target is a group of wealthy traders and pilgrims, travelling to Canterbury; they will be passing through Gad's Hill, an ideal spot for waylaying travellers, early tomorrow morning.

Falstaff is keen to take advantage of this lucrative opportunity, but Hal declines. Poins assures Falstaff that his young friend can be persuaded, and the knight sets off for Eastcheap, the site of his favourite tavern.

Poins now explains to the prince that his plan is not simply to rob the travellers, but to play a trick on Falstaff. He and Hal will keep their distance from the scene of the robbery: Falstaff and his other accomplices will go ahead with the crime, but Poins and Hal, in disguise, will then rob them in turn.

Falstaff is a notorious coward and braggart. Poins is certain that he will not put up a fight, and robbing him will be child's play. However, the real entertainment will be in hearing Falstaff's version of events at the tavern in the evening, not realising the identity of his assailants.

> *Poins:* The virtue of this jest will be the incomprehensible lies that this same fat rogue will tell us when we meet at supper, how thirty at least he fought with, what wards,[1] what blows, what extremities he endured ...

> [1] *defensive strategies*

Hal cannot resist the idea, and he agrees to go along with the plan.

A bright future

Poins leaves, and the prince, now alone, reflects on the company he is keeping. He is well aware that his current way of life is dissolute and disreputable, but he assures himself that it will not last much longer. Soon he will turn his back on this depravity, and become the upright, honourable man he was meant to be. The contrast with his old life will make him all the more respected:

> *Prince:* ... herein will I imitate the sun,
> Who doth permit the base contagious clouds
> To smother up his beauty from the world,
> That, when he please again to be himself,
> Being wanted he may be more wonder'd at ...

After all, he reasons, it is unexpected and infrequent events that capture our attention and give us the greatest pleasure:

> *Prince:* If all the year were playing holidays,
> To sport would be as tedious as to work ...

He looks forward to the time when, casting his old ways aside, he will dazzle those around him like the royal heir that he is.

Hotspur explains himself

Henry Percy, summoned by the king, has come to Windsor castle. With him are his father, Earl of Northumberland, and his uncle, Earl of Worcester. The king is angrily reprimanding young Percy, who has not handed over the Scottish prisoners captured at Holmedon. He will no longer endure the young man's arrogance, and blames himself for allowing his tolerant disposition to override the authority required of a king.

King: ... You tread upon my patience: but be sure
                  I will from henceforth rather be myself,[1]
                  Mighty, and to be fear'd, than my condition,[2]
                  Which hath been smooth as oil, soft as young down ...

[1] *what I am as a king*
[2] *what I am by nature*

Worcester interjects, reminding the king that the Percy family played a significant role in helping the king to overthrow Richard the Second and to achieve the power that he now enjoys. This infuriates the king even more, and he dismisses Worcester from his presence.

Northumberland now addresses the king, taking a more conciliatory tone. His son is not guilty of the arrogant disobedience of which he is accused, claims Northumberland: the message delivered to the king after the battle was distorted, either through malice or misunderstanding.

At this point Hotspur launches into a vigorous, colourful account of the events following the battle of Holmedon. He recalls the arrival of the king's messenger on the battlefield:

Hotspur: ... I remember, when the fight was done,
                When I was dry with rage, and extreme toil,
                Breathless and faint, leaning upon my sword,
                Came there a certain lord, neat and trimly dress'd,
                Fresh as a bridegroom, and his chin new reap'd
                Show'd like a stubble-land at harvest-home.
                He was perfumed like a milliner ...

The man clearly found the whole business of war distasteful, complaining about the sight and smell of the corpses and the noise of the guns, and he prattled foolishly about the best cure for wounds and his own ambition to be a soldier.

At some point, Hotspur recalls, the man mentioned the prisoners, but by this time Hotspur was so infuriated by his ridiculous, fastidious manner that he could barely bring himself to speak to him. He no doubt gave the man an awkward, unhelpful answer, Hotspur admits, but this was surely understandable in the bloody aftermath of the battle, and should not be taken for disobedience to the king.

The king issues an ultimatum

The king's trusted adviser Sir Walter Blunt urges him to accept Hotspur's explanation. But the king is far from satisfied, for Hotspur, whatever excuses he may make, is still refusing to hand over the prisoners. His wife's brother is Edmund Mortimer, who led the campaign against Owen Glendower, and who is now a prisoner of the Welsh. Hotspur has demanded that the king pay the ransom required to free his brother-in-law Mortimer before he will release the prisoners captured at Holmedon.

The king is furious. Not only is Mortimer a coward who led hundreds of Englishmen to their deaths; he has, since his capture, married Glendower's daughter. As far as the king is concerned, Mortimer is a traitor, and it is unthinkable that his ransom should be paid.

Hotspur angrily defends his brother-in-law. Far from being a coward, Mortimer actually tackled the fearsome Glendower in single combat, claims Hotspur, receiving severe wounds in the process. The king is scornful of this claim. Growing ever more impatient, he makes a final demand to Hotspur for the captured prisoners; there will be serious consequences if he disobeys. The king takes his leave without giving Hotspur any further opportunity for dissent.

Hotspur is on the verge of pursuing the king and risking his life by giving a direct refusal to the king's demand, but his father Northumberland urges him to pause. The young man remains where he is, but the dispute over Mortimer has infuriated him. His brother-in-law is a far better man than the king, who has shown no gratitude to the Percy family for their support when, as Henry Bolingbroke, he seized the crown from King Richard:

Hotspur: ... I will lift the down-trod Mortimer
As high in the air as this unthankful King,
As this ingrate and canker'd[1] Bolingbroke.

[1] *corrupt, diseased*

... this ingrate and canker'd Bolingbroke.

Henry IV is known to have suffered from a disfiguring skin disease and other health problems, particularly towards the end of his life. Many regarded this as divine retribution for usurping his cousin, Richard II:

"For the whole of his time as king, Henry was forced to beat off rivals and rebels. Troubles of one sort or another worried him till he died: arguments in parliament, fighting along the Welsh and Scottish borders; plots and skirmishes. Executions were constantly necessary, simply to keep himself in power ... The strain of events seriously undermined his health. He contracted a troublesome skin disease, eczema or perhaps leprosy. Rumour had it that this illness was the revenge of God ..."

David Hilliam, *Kings, Queens, Bones and Bastards*, 1998

A shock for Hotspur

In the meantime the Earl of Worcester, Hotspur's uncle, has returned. He asks his brother Northumberland what has caused the young man's fury. When he learns of the king's refusal to ransom Mortimer, he is not surprised:

> *Worcester:* I cannot blame him: was he not proclaim'd,
> By Richard that dead is, the next of blood?
> *Northumberland:* He was, I heard the proclamation …

Overhearing their conversation, Hotspur is stunned. He had not realised that the previous king, Richard the Second, had named Mortimer – who indeed had a valid claim to the throne – as his successor. This explains why King Henry, who deposed Richard, is refusing to liberate Mortimer, preferring to let him live as a virtual exile in Wales.

Hotspur's resentment towards the king grows stronger and stronger as he considers the implications of what he has just heard. His family, the Percys, played a major part in Richard's downfall, and many despise them for it; yet all their efforts were for a man who was undeserving of the crown, and who is utterly ungrateful and even hostile towards those who supported him. The family's honour has been lost in an unworthy cause.

> *Hotspur:* Shall it for shame be spoken in these days,
> Or fill up chronicles in time to come,
> That men of your nobility and power
> Did gage them both[1] in an unjust behalf
> (As both of you, God pardon it, have done)
> To put down Richard, that sweet lovely rose,
> And plant this thorn, this canker[2] Bolingbroke?

> [1] *pledge both your nobility and your power*
> [2] *dog-rose; also a disease affecting roses, or an ulcer*

Their honour must be regained at all costs, insists Hotspur, by now in a state of furious agitation: they must take revenge on the king, who holds them in contempt, and who in any case is planning their deaths.

> *"In the opening scenes two issues make their way into the foreground. One is the fact that medieval warfare was in large part a ransom racket: you took noblemen prisoner in battle, and then their tenants had to put up enough money to buy them back ... The other is the fact that Edmund Mortimer, Earl of March, has in some respects a better claim to the throne than Henry IV has ..."*
>
> Northrop Frye, *On Shakespeare*, 1986

Worcester tries to interrupt the young man's tirade. He has a very serious proposition to put to him, he explains, but Hotspur, caught up in his passionate outburst on the theme of injustice, revenge and honour, refuses to listen. Neither his father nor his uncle can communicate with him in this state:

Northumberland: Imagination of some great exploit
  Drives him beyond the bounds of patience.
Hotspur: By heaven, methinks it were an easy leap
  To pluck bright honour from the pale-fac'd moon,
  Or dive into the bottom of the deep,
  Where fathom-line could never touch the ground,
  And pluck up drowned honour by the locks ...
Worcester: He apprehends a world of figures[1] here,
  But not the form of what he should attend ...

[1] *he is grasping at imaginary notions*

Northumberland and Worcester start to lose patience with the young man. Meanwhile, in Hotspur's imagination he sees himself tormenting the king and even poisoning his son Hal. Then his mind moves on restlessly to the time when, as a youth, he first met Bolingbroke, who flattered him and promised him a bright future. Eventually he returns to the present, and allows Worcester to set out his proposal.

A rebellion is planned

Hotspur must release his Scottish prisoners without ransom, explains Worcester, and ally himself with the defeated Scottish army led by the Earl of Douglas. Meanwhile, Northumberland is to gain the confidence of the Archbishop of York, whose brother was executed by King Henry, and who is prepared to take up arms against the king. Worcester himself will go to Wales and make contact with Mortimer and Glendower.

Worcester is adamant that the Percy family is in imminent danger from the king, who knows he is in their debt and resents them for it. For their own safety they must confront him: and this triple alliance of armies from Scotland, York and Wales will surely prove invincible. Hotspur is eager to return to the battlefield:

Hotspur: ... O, let the hours be short,
          Till fields, and blows, and groans applaud our sport!

The play's restless movement from one group of characters to another highlights the differences between their worlds. But sometimes we cannot help noticing parallels too, even if they are unstated: for example, the king's ambition to go on a crusade to Jerusalem; Falstaff's ambition to carry out the perfect robbery; and Hotspur's ambition to overthrow the king and regain his family's honour.

"The play brings before us three contrasting environments at once, each with a commanding personality. The court is Henry's domain; the tavern is Falstaff's; the feudal countryside is Hotspur's ... within this simple framework, Shakespeare accomplishes an articulation of complementary images, cross-references, and ironic contrasts that is without parallel in the history of English stage comedy."

Maynard Mack, Introduction to the Signet Classic edition of *Henry IV, Part 1*, 1986

An early start

Outside an inn in Rochester, two carriers are preparing to set
out for London with their assorted goods. It is nearly four in
the morning, and they are anxious to load their pack-horses
and leave. They shout impatiently to the stableman to get their
horses ready. The two of them agree on the standard of their
accommodation:

Second Carrier: I think this be the most villainous house in all
London road for fleas, I am stung like a tench.[1]
First Carrier: Like a tench! By the mass, there is ne'er a king
christen could be better bit than I have been since
the first cock.[2]
Second Carrier: Why, they will allow us ne'er a jordan,[3] and
then we leak in your[4] chimney, and your chamber-lye[5]
breeds fleas like a loach.[6]

[1] *a fish with scaly, speckled skin*
[2] *midnight*
[3] *chamber-pot*
[4] *the*
[5] *urine*
[6] *fish reputed to produce large numbers of parasites*

Gadshill, the highwayman who has planned the robbery in
which Falstaff, Hal and Poins are to take part, now comes into
the inn-yard. He casually asks the carriers when they are
leaving for London, but they are suspicious of him and answer
evasively. However, as the carriers leave, Gadshill overhears
as one of them mentions that some gentlemen with valuable
property will be travelling with them.

Gadshill calls for the chamberlain, a servant at the inn who
also works as Gadshill's informer. He has good news for the
highwayman, confirming the carrier's overheard remark:

Chamberlain: It holds current[1] that I told you yesternight:
there's a franklin[2] in the Wild of Kent hath brought
three hundred marks with him in gold ...

[1] *is still true*
[2] *wealthy farmer, landowner*

The franklin, along with some other prosperous travellers, will be leaving shortly. Gadshill is pleased with the information, and promises the chamberlain a share of the loot. He boasts that he will be joined in his enterprise by men of high status, higher than the chamberlain can imagine; even if things go wrong, he and his accomplices will escape justice.

Gadshill needs to hurry to the agreed location ahead of the travellers, and he calls for his horse.

Danger on the highway
II, ii

Near the road from Rochester to London, the robbers are gathering in the darkness. Falstaff, Hal and Poins have arrived; two further accomplices, Peto and Bardolph, are in the vicinity, as is Gadshill, who has travelled from the inn in Rochester.

Prince Hal and Poins watch as Falstaff struggles to the site of the robbery on foot; Poins has taken his horse and hidden it. The corpulent old knight hates walking, and Poins' trick has put him in a bad temper.

> *Falstaff:* I am accursed to rob in that thief's company …
> eight yards of uneven ground is threescore and ten
> miles afoot with me, and the stony-hearted villains
> know it well enough. A plague upon it when thieves
> cannot be true one to another!

Hal approaches, and tells Falstaff to be quiet and put his ear to the ground. Falstaff refuses, claiming that he is so exhausted that he would not be able to haul himself up again.

While Falstaff is complaining about his ill-treatment, Gadshill and Bardolph emerge from the darkness. They report that there are at least eight travellers on their way, with plenty of money between them. They tell their companions to put on their masks; the travellers are coming down the hill towards them.

Hal suggests that four of them – Falstaff, Gadshill, Bardolph and Peto – confront the travellers, while he and Poins wait further down the hill in case they escape. Poins does Falstaff the favour of telling him where his horse is hidden, and then he and Hal slip away into the night.

Meanwhile, the travellers from Rochester have dismounted at the top of the hill and are making their way down on foot. As they pass, the thieves jump out into the road and order them to stop. While the thieves busy themselves robbing the terrified men and tying them up so they cannot escape, Falstaff hurls a stream of insults at them, accusing them of being overfed parasites who bully younger men like himself:

> *Travellers:* Jesus bless us!
> *Falstaff:* Strike, down with them, cut the villains' throats!
> Ah, whoreson caterpillars, bacon-fed knaves, they
> hate us youth! Down with them, fleece them!

When they have made their getaway, the four robbers find a secluded spot, lay out the spoils, and proceed to share them between themselves. Falstaff remarks on the cowardice of the other two men, who were not present at the robbery, unaware that Poins and Hal, in disguise, are observing them.

The two spectators now draw their weapons and threaten the robbers, demanding their money. Falstaff makes a brief attempt to fight back, but the four of them soon scatter into the night. Poins and Hal collect the loot, delighted with the outcome. Hal is particularly amused by the thought of Falstaff as he retreats, exhausted and demoralised:

> *Prince:* ... Falstaff sweats to death,
> And lards the lean earth as he walks along.
> Were't not for laughing I should pity him.

Hotspur grows impatient

Hotspur is at Warkworth Castle, the base of the Percy family in the north of England. He is reading a letter, with growing frustration at its contents. It becomes clear that the letter is from a nobleman who is refusing, courteously but firmly, to join Hotspur in his planned rebellion.

> *Hotspur:* ... "The purpose you undertake is dangerous" – Why, that's certain; 'tis dangerous to take a cold, to sleep, to drink; but I tell you, my lord fool, out of this nettle, danger, we pluck this flower, safety. "The purpose you undertake is dangerous, the friends you have named uncertain, the time itself unsorted,[1] and your whole plot too light, for the counterpoise of so great an opposition." Say you so, say you so?
>
> [1] *unsuitable*

Hotspur is exasperated at the man's failure to grasp how sound and strong the plot is, and at his lack of imagination and courage:

> *Hotspur:* ... what a lack-brain is this! By the Lord, our plot is a good plot, as ever was laid, our friends true and constant ... what a frosty-spirited rogue is this! ... Is there not my father, my uncle, and myself? Lord Edmund Mortimer, my Lord[1] of York, and Owen Glendower? Is there not besides the Douglas? Have I not all their letters to meet me in arms by the ninth of the next month, and are they not some of them set forward already?
>
> [1] *the Archbishop*

The man may well inform the king of the planned rebellion, Hotspur realises, and he scolds himself for having invited such an insipid character to join the plot. Hotspur quickly shrugs off the thought: it simply means that action is all the more urgent.

> *Hotspur:* ... Hang him, let him tell the King, we are prepared: I will set forward tonight.

At this point Kate, Hotspur's wife, joins him. She is worried about him; in recent days he has been moody and lost in thought. His sleep is disturbed and he seems to be haunted by obsessive dreams of war.

> *Lady Percy:* Tell me, sweet lord, what is't that takes from thee
> Thy stomach,[1] pleasure, and thy golden sleep?
> … In thy faint slumbers I by thee have watch'd,
> And heard thee murmur tales of iron wars,
> Speak terms of manage[2] to thy bounding steed,
> Cry "Courage! To the field!" And thou hast talk'd
> Of sallies, and retires, of trenches, tents,
> Of palisadoes, frontiers, parapets …

[1] *appetite*
[2] *commands*

She appeals to him to tell her what is on his mind, and why he is leaving so urgently, but Hotspur is busy making preparations for his departure, and answers teasingly. She suspects that he is getting involved in some sort of plot, and is determined to find out:

> *Lady Percy:* But hear you, my lord.
> *Hotspur:* What say'st thou, my lady?
> *Lady Percy:* What is it carries you away?
> *Hotspur:* Why, my horse, my love, my horse.
> *Lady Percy:* Out, you mad-headed ape!
> A weasel hath not such a deal of spleen[1]
> As you are toss'd with. In faith,
> I'll know your business, Harry, that I will;
> I fear my brother Mortimer doth stir
> About his title,[2] and hath sent for you
> To line[3] his enterprise.

[1] *awkwardness, contrariness*
[2] *his entitlement to the throne*
[3] *strengthen*

Hotspur continues to evade her questions. However trustworthy she may be, he cannot risk letting her know of his plans:

> Hotspur: But hark you, Kate,
> I must not have you henceforth question me
> Whither I go, nor reason whereabout:
> Whither I must, I must; and, to conclude,
> This evening must I leave you, gentle Kate.

He promises his wife that she can join him tomorrow.

Hal is in high spirits

II, iv

Hal and Poins are spending the evening in the Boar's Head tavern, the favorite haunt of Falstaff and his associates. Hal tells Poins that he has been down in the cellar, drinking with a group of simple-minded serving-staff.

> Poins: Where hast been, Hal?
> Prince: With three or four loggerheads,[1] amongst three or
>   fourscore hogsheads.[2] I have sounded the very
>   base-string of humility. Sirrah, I am sworn brother
>   to a leash[3] of drawers,[4] and can call them all by their
>   christen names, as Tom, Dick, and Francis. They take
>   it already upon their salvation, that though I be but
>   Prince of Wales, yet I am the king of courtesy, and
>   tell me flatly I am no proud Jack like Falstaff …

[1] *simpletons*
[2] *large barrels of wine or ale*
[3] *trio*
[4] *those who 'draw' drink from the barrels and
serve it; tapsters*

They regard him as a fine drinking-companion, he reports proudly, and in the brief time he spent with them he picked up some of their slang and customs around drinking.

Prince: … I am so good a proficient in one quarter of an hour that I can drink with any tinker in his own language during my life. I tell thee, Ned, thou hast lost much honour that thou wert not with me in this action[1] …

[1] *encounter, engagement*

Hal is particularly amused by the junior wine-server, named Francis, and his incessant cry of "Anon, anon, sir!" as customers call for drinks. While they wait for Falstaff's arrival, Hal teases Francis by bombarding him with confusing questions while Poins, in a different room, repeatedly cries out for service. Eventually the boy is so baffled that he no longer knows which way to turn or what to say. The innkeeper scolds Francis for inattention, and tells the prince that Falstaff is about to come in.

In the noisy, convivial atmosphere of the tavern, Hal is in a cheerful mood. His outlook on life is nothing like Hotspur's, he jokes:

Prince: I am not yet of Percy's mind, the Hotspur of the north, he that kills me some six or seven dozen of Scots at a breakfast, washes his hands, and says to his wife, "Fie upon this quiet life, I want work."

Shakespeare's history plays – unlike his comedies, tragedies and later plays – have relatively few prominent female roles. For one playwright, actress and critic of Georgian times, *Henry IV* was too aggressively masculine to be successful:

"This is a play which all men admire, and which most women dislike. Many revolting expressions in the comic parts, much boisterous courage in some of the graver scenes, together with Falstaff's unwieldy person, offend every female auditor."

Elizabeth Inchbald, *The British Theatre*, 1808

An unreliable narrative

Falstaff now arrives, along with the other unsuccessful robbers. The loss of his loot has put him in a foul temper. He is sorry for himself, and angry with the world in general.

Falstaff: … there lives not three good men unhanged in England, and one of them is fat, and grows old …

When Falstaff sees Hal and Poins, he is even more irate; they failed to support their friends when, after the robbery, the four of them were set upon by a great gang of thieves who stole their loot. As predicted, his version of events bears little resemblance to the truth.

Falstaff: I am a rogue if I were not at half-sword[1] with a dozen of them two hours together. I have scaped by miracle. I am eight times thrust through the doublet,[2] four through the hose,[3] my buckler[4] cut through and through, my sword hacked like a handsaw …

[1] *half a sword's length; close quarters*
[2] *jacket*
[3] *breeches*
[4] *small shield*

To prove his point, Falstaff produces his battered sword with a flourish. Encouraged by Hal, Falstaff continues with his fantastical account of the fight, accompanied by a demonstration of his prowess.

Prince: Pray god you have not murdered some of them.
Falstaff: Nay, that's past praying for, I have peppered two of them. Two I am sure have paid, two rogues in buckram[1] suits … here I lay,[2] and thus I bore my point.[3] Four rogues in buckram let drive at me –
Prince: What, four? Thou saidst but two even now.
Falstaff: Four, Hal, I told thee four.

[1] *rough cloth (Hal and Poins' disguises were made of buckram)*
[2] *this was my posture of defence*
[3] *sword*

Hal and Poins listen with delight as Falstaff's description becomes ever more ridiculous. Eventually Hal points out the absurdity of his tale, and accuses him of lying, adding a colourful stream of insults:

> *Prince:* These lies are like their father that begets them, gross as a mountain, open, palpable. Why, thou clay-brained guts, thou knotty-pated[1] fool, thou whoreson obscene greasy tallow-catch[2] ...
>
> [1] *block-headed*
> [2] *pan to collect fat dripping from roasting meat*

Falstaff insists that he is telling the truth. He in turn launches a barrage of insults at the lanky young prince.

> *Falstaff:* 'Sblood, you starveling, you eel-skin, you dried neat's-tongue,[1] you bull's-pizzle ...
>
> [1] *ox-tongue*

Exhausted by his angry rant, Falstaff pauses to catch his breath. Now the prince reveals the truth: that there were just two assailants, himself and Poins, and that the four robbers ran off without a fight, leaving the plunder behind. Hal has the stolen hoard here in the inn to prove it.

Falstaff's air of righteous indignation evaporates. But instead of remorse or discomfort, the old knight is suddenly jovial. Of course he recognised the prince, he declares cheerfully. When Hal and Poins appeared after the robbery, he had to repress his natural courage and ferocity. Just as the lion is reputed never to harm those of royal blood, Falstaff's noble instincts prevented him from harming the heir to the throne.

> *Falstaff:* Why, thou knowest I am as valiant as Hercules: but beware instinct – the lion will not touch the true prince ... I was now a coward on instinct: I shall think the better of myself, and thee, during my life – I for a valiant lion, and thou for a true prince. But by the Lord, lads, I am glad you have the money.

> *"Falstaff is allow'd by every body to be a Master-piece ... If there be any Fault in the Draught he has made of this lewd old Fellow, it is that tho' he has made him a Thief, Lying, Cowardly, Vain-glorious, and in short every way Vicious, yet he has given him so much Wit as to make him almost too agreeable."*
>
> Nicholas Rowe, *Some Account of the Life, &c. of Mr. William Shakespear*, 1709

The king summons his son

The hostess of the tavern enters, and tells Hal that a nobleman, sent by the king, has come to speak with him. The prince is not interested, and he sends Falstaff off to get rid of the unwanted visitor.

In Falstaff's absence, the prince questions Bardolph and Peto about the robbery. Embarrassed, they confirm that Falstaff persuaded them to hack at their swords to make them look as if they had been used in combat. He even got them to provoke nosebleeds by thrusting straws up their noses, and to smear their clothes with the resulting blood.

Falstaff returns with news from the messenger. An uprising against the king is under way; forces from all around the country are uniting in rebellion. Hal has been ordered to see his father in the morning.

Falstaff and Hal are interested in the news, but not particularly shaken by it. The security of the kingdom is the last thing on their minds; in fact, civil war has its advantages.

Falstaff: ... thy father's beard is turned white with the news; you may buy land now as cheap as stinking mackerel.

Prince: Why then, it is like if there come a hot June, and this civil buffeting hold,[1] we shall buy maidenheads as they buy hob-nails, by the hundreds.[2]

[1] *if this civil war goes ahead*
[2] *when all the men go off to war, there will be no shortage of willing young women*

Eventually Falstaff points out that the situation holds some significance for the prince. But Hal remains unmoved; he does not have Falstaff's lion-like nature, he remarks ironically.

> *Falstaff:* Thou being heir apparent, could the world pick thee
> out three such enemies again, as that fiend Douglas,
> that spirit Percy, and that devil Glendower? Art thou
> not horribly afraid? Doth not thy blood thrill[1] at it?
>
> *Prince:* Not a whit, i'faith, I lack some of thy instinct.

[1] *shiver*

The prince will receive a severe scolding from his father in the morning, warns Falstaff. He suggests that they rehearse the scene immediately so that Hal can prepare some answers.

The two of them hastily collect a few props, and Falstaff launches enthusiastically into an impromptu performance as King Henry. He gives a colourful, rambling but eloquent speech admonishing the prince for wasting his youth, and ruining his reputation, by spending so much time in depraved company. He has, on the other hand, noticed one of his companions who can exert a positive influence on the young man:

> *Falstaff:* And yet there is a virtuous man whom I have often
> noted in thy company ... A goodly portly man, i'faith,
> and a corpulent; of a cheerful look, a pleasing eye,
> and a most noble carriage; and, as I think, his age
> some fifty, or by'r lady inclining to threescore ...

At the end of his high-flown speech, Falstaff's king comes down to earth:

> *Falstaff:* And tell me now, thou naughty varlet, tell me where
> hast thou been this month?

This is not how the king speaks, complains Hal. He decides to take over as king, while Falstaff plays the prince. The new king immediately berates the prince for spending time with a bloated, corrupt, drink-sodden old ruffian. Falstaff, as prince, defends himself eloquently, but the imaginary king is unmoved.

> *Falstaff:*   If sack and sugar be a fault, God help the wicked!
>   If to be old and merry be a sin, then many an old host
>   that I know is damned ... for sweet Jack Falstaff, kind
>   Jack Falstaff, true Jack Falstaff, valiant Jack Falstaff ...
>   banish not him thy Harry's company, banish[1] plump
>   Jack, and banish all the world.
>
> *Prince:*   I do, I will.

[1] *if you banish*

I do, I will.

"Immediately after Hal's quietly menacing words, we have the stage-direction 'A knocking heard'. We know that knocking. It is the hand of the cold reality which tells us we must search our pockets and pay up. It is the knocking on the gate in Macbeth.*"*

John Wain, *The Living World of Shakespeare*, 1964

Falstaff is pursued

At this point Bardolph runs in. The sheriff is at the door, he exclaims, with a band of citizens. Falstaff silences him, impatient to continue with the play; as prince, he has much more to say on behalf of his companion. However, the hostess now rushes in and confirms Bardolph's message. The sheriff intends to search the tavern. Hal tells Falstaff to hide behind the tapestry hanging on a wall nearby.

The sheriff comes in, accompanied by one of the carriers who witnessed the robbery near Rochester. The identity of one of the suspects quickly becomes clear:

Sheriff:	... pardon me, my lord. A hue and cry[1] Hath follow'd certain men unto this house.
Prince:	What men?
Sheriff:	One of them is well known, my gracious lord, A gross fat man.
Carrier:	As fat as butter.

[1] *a group of witnesses and bystanders who pursue a criminal*

The prince replies courteously. He knows the man, but assures the sheriff that he is not present − in fact, he is currently employed on the prince's own business. He promises to send him to the sheriff the following day, and to make sure that he takes responsibility for any crime he may have committed. The sheriff is satisfied, and leaves the tavern.

Hal and Peto call out to Falstaff that it is safe to emerge from his hiding-place. There is no answer, and they pull back the wall-hanging to reveal Falstaff fast asleep and snoring loudly. The prince asks Peto to look in his friend's pockets. There is nothing but a few papers, including a tavern bill for a little bread, a chicken, and more than two gallons of wine. Hal is appalled and amused at the same time.

It is very late now, and they leave Falstaff to sleep in his hiding-place. Hal's thoughts turn towards the impending conflict with the rebels. All of them will be involved, he reflects, even Falstaff:

> Prince: We must all to the wars ... I'll procure this fat rogue a charge of foot,[1] and I know his death will be a march of twelve score.[2]
>
> [1] *I'll put him in charge of a company of infantry*
> [2] *even a short march will be the death of him*

Hal mentions to Peto that the travellers who were robbed will be repaid with interest. With that, he retires to bed; it is very late now, and he will be meeting the king in the morning.

Twenty-five years after Shakespeare's death, civil war between the English Parliament and the Crown was looming. In 1642, the London theatres were temporarily closed by order of the puritan-dominated Parliament, which decreed that:

"Publike Sports doe not well agree with publike Calamities."

Two years later, the closure was declared permanent. The Globe, where many of Shakespeare's plays had first been performed, was demolished, and the site used for housing.

It was to be fifteen years before theatrical performances were again legalized, with the restoration of the monarchy in 1660. However, in the intervening years the performing arts had not died out altogether. Brief, comical sketches known as 'drolls' – usually adapted from old plays – were presented, often surreptitiously, in taverns and at fairs.

One of the most popular drolls consisted of a collection of scenes, mainly from *Henry IV*, which featured Falstaff. The piece was called *The Bouncing Knight*.

A clash of personalities

Hotspur and his uncle, the Earl of Worcester, have travelled to Wales. They have come to meet Mortimer, the rival claimant to the throne of England, and his former enemy, the Welsh rebel leader Owen Glendower.

Mortimer, brother to Hotspur's wife and now married to Glendower's daughter, is optimistic about their prospects.

> *Mortimer:* These promises are fair, the parties[1] sure,
> And our induction[2] full of prosperous hope.
>
> [1] *participants, allies*
> [2] *beginning*

Glendower is aware that Hotspur is a source of vexation to King Henry, and he respects the young man for this. Hotspur returns the compliment, knowing that Glendower is hated and feared by the English king. Quite rightly, says Glendower, who believes himself to have been marked out at birth as a force of nature:

> *Glendower:*   … at my nativity,
> The front[1] of heaven was full of fiery shapes,
> Of burning cressets,[2] and at my birth
> The frame and huge foundation of the earth
> Shak'd like a coward.
>
> [1] *face*
> [2] *beacons*

Hotspur is scornful of the Welshman's melodramatic description. Earth tremors are common, he insists, and such phenomena have straightforward natural causes. Glendower is offended, but manages, with difficulty, to restrain his temper. Once more he asserts that the disturbances in nature accompanying his birth were portents of an extraordinary existence: and they have proved to be true. No one in the land can match him for his understanding of the supernatural world and the complexities of magic. Hotspur remains scathing of Glendower's supposed mystical abilities, and Mortimer tries to quieten the young man so that they can make progress with negotiations.

Eventually Glendower brings their attention to the map of the kingdom. This shows how the country is to be divided between the three parties once King Henry is successfully removed. It has been settled that the north of England will go to Percy and the south to Mortimer, while Wales becomes an independent nation under Owen Glendower.

The final agreement over the division of the country must be signed and sealed today: tomorrow Mortimer, Hotspur and Worcester will gather at Shrewsbury, where they will unite with Hotspur's father, Northumberland, and their allies from Scotland. Glendower, who will not be needed immediately, is to assemble his army over the coming days.

The spectacle of the rebels calmly studying a map and dividing up the nation would have shocked an Elizabethan audience.

The first accurate map of England had been commissioned in the 1570s by Queen Elizabeth's senior advisers. It was produced by Christopher Saxton, who spent the following eight years surveying the nation and producing a county-by-county atlas as well as an overall map of the country. This new map of England, so familiar to us now, held a potent symbolism for the Elizabethans.

"Maps were instruments of power ... To have in their hands a picture of every corner of England, revealing the exact location of each town and village, charting the course of each river and road: this was the dream of the men of power who set Saxton to work on his monumental surveying expedition. The map offered such a new way of seeing England that Saxton's atlas grew into one of the most powerful icons of the age. The reign of Queen Elizabeth was the first time anyone had ever seen the precise outline that is so familiar to us from school geography lessons and nightly television weather charts ... Thanks to Saxton, the Elizabethans were the first English people to have a clear sense of the physical shape of their own nation. And that gave them a new sense of belonging."

Jonathan Bate, *Soul of the Age*, 2008

A boundary dispute

Hotspur looks more closely at the map, and finds a problem. His share of the country is smaller than the other two, he argues; the winding river Trent deprives him of a significant area of valuable land. To put things right, he intends to dam up the river and alter its course.

The idea is ridiculous, says Glendower; while Mortimer points out that a different stretch of the meandering river cuts off a similar area of land from his own share, to Hotspur's advantage.

Hotspur's uncle suggests a smaller alteration to the Trent, but Glendower is adamant; the river must be left untouched. He and Hotspur face up to one another defiantly. Perhaps Glendower should be speaking Welsh, suggests Hotspur, so that his objections could be ignored. Glendower points out that he is perfectly comfortable with the English language.

> *Glendower:* I can speak English, lord, as well as you,
> For I was train'd up in the English court,
> Where being but young I framed to the harp
> Many an English ditty lovely well,
> And gave the tongue a helpful ornament [1] –
> A virtue that was never seen in you.
>
> [1] *made the language beautiful by the addition of music*

Hotspur heartily agrees that he takes no pleasure in singing or poetry. He finds the affectation and repetitiveness of ballads and verses unbearable:

> *Hotspur:*   … 'Tis like the forc'd gait of a shuffling nag. [1]
>
> [1] *uncomfortable motion of a plodding old horse*

The mood lightens, and Glendower agrees to Hotspur's request to change the course of the river. Hotspur, for his part, immediately forgets the quarrel. The land is not important, he claims; he cannot help his natural inclination to strive for the best possible result.

> Glendower: Come, you shall have Trent turn'd.
> Hotspur: I do not care, I'll give thrice so much land
>   To any well-deserving friend:
>   But in the way of bargain, mark ye me,
>   I'll cavil on the ninth part of a hair.

The final agreement over the division of the kingdom can now be drawn up, and will soon be ready for signing; Mortimer and the Percys will then set off for Shrewsbury. Glendower leaves to fetch the men's wives. He predicts that his daughter will be distraught at the departure of her beloved husband Mortimer.

As soon as Glendower is out of the room, Mortimer and Worcester rebuke Hotspur for his headstrong attitude towards their Welsh ally. Hotspur explains that he finds the man's long-winded mysticism intensely irritating.

> Hotspur: I cannot choose; sometime he angers me
>   With telling me of the moldwarp[1] and the ant,
>   Of the dreamer Merlin and his prophecies,
>   And of a dragon and a finless fish,
>   A clip-wing'd griffin and a moulten raven …

[1] mole

Mortimer replies that his father-in-law is an admirable, learned man. He is also generous and brave, and he holds Hotspur in high regard. Glendower has shown enormous self-restraint in tolerating the young man's belligerence, says Mortimer; he may not be so indulgent in future.

Hotspur's uncle Worcester, too, criticises him for his wilful, argumentative behaviour. While it may be an aspect of his undoubted courage, most people will see it as arrogance and rudeness, and it is likely to lose him friends. Hotspur thanks him sarcastically for the lesson; perhaps good manners will win them the war.

> *"Hotspur parallels Falstaff in his scornful opposition of body to words; both man of action and man of inertia are paradoxically akin in this ... The difference between the two figures is that Hotspur is an old-style idealist who desires a language adequate to action and vice versa; Falstaff has not the slightest wish to integrate the two, but flourishes in the gulf between them."*
>
> Terry Eagleton, *William Shakespeare*, 1986

A musical interlude

Glendower returns, accompanied by his daughter and by Hotspur's wife, Lady Percy. As Glendower expected, his daughter is tearful at the departure of her husband Mortimer. She speaks no English, and Mortimer, who speaks no Welsh, asks Glendower to interpret as he reassures her that she will be able to join him soon.

Mortimer, on the verge of tears himself, promises his wife that he will learn her language. She wishes to sing to him before he goes:

> *Glendower:* She bids you on the wanton[1] rushes lay you down,
> And rest your gentle head upon her lap,
> And she will sing the song that pleaseth you,
> And on your eyelids crown[2] the god of sleep ...
>
> [1] *luxurious*
> [2] *give sovereignty to*

Lady Percy and Hotspur, by contrast, tease one another playfully. Hotspur is not looking forward to the singing.

> *Lady Percy:* Lie still, ye thief, and hear the lady sing in Welsh.
> *Hotspur:*　　I had rather hear Lady my brach[1] howl in Irish.
>
> [1] *hound*

Mortimer lies drowsily in his wife's lap as she sings to him. Hotspur light-heartedly urges his wife to sing too, but she refuses. He soon becomes impatient, and prepares to leave. Mortimer, on the other hand, has to be roused to action.

> *Glendower:* Come, come, Lord Mortimer, you are as slow
> As hot Lord Percy is on fire to go:
> By this our book is drawn[1] – we'll but seal,[2]
> And then to horse immediately.

> [1] *our final agreement has been drawn up by now*
> [2] *sign and verify it*

The prince gives his word   III, ii

Prince Harry has come to meet his father as instructed. The king makes it clear at once that he is dismayed at his son's debauched behaviour. The prince is a man of royal blood, and the only explanation for his depravity and dishonour is surely some form of divine retribution for the king's own failings.

> *King:* I know not whether God will have it so
> For some displeasing service I have done,
> That in his secret doom[1] out of my blood[2]
> He'll breed revengement and a scourge[3] for me …

> [1] *unknowable judgement*
> [2] *from my heirs*
> [3] *chastisement, punishment*

The prince freely acknowledges that he has committed misdeeds, but suggests respectfully that not all the stories that have reached the king are true; amongst the followers of great men such as himself, there are inevitably many who wish to spread false rumours for their own ends.

The king is perplexed by the fact that his son is so different from his forebears in his tastes and conduct. Despite his royal ancestry, he takes no part in government – his place on the king's council having been taken by his younger brother – and has thus failed to gain the friendship of many important, influential people in the king's court. Even now, many people believe that his reign, when it comes, will be a failure.

King Henry remembers how, as an ambitious young man, he understood the importance of maintaining a degree of remoteness:

> King: By being seldom seen, I could not stir
> But like a comet I was wonder'd at,
> That men would tell their children, "This is he!"

King Richard, by contrast, spent his time courting popularity, and was frequently seen amidst noisy crowds. Eventually people of all classes wearied of him; and when Henry challenged him for the crown, his own aura of mystery attracted countless supporters. Becoming tearful, the king warns Harry that he has become like King Richard.

> King: … thou hast lost thy princely privilege
> With vile participation.[1] Not an eye
> But is a-weary of thy common sight,
> Save mine, which hath desir'd to see thee more,
> Which now doth that I would not have it do,
> Make blind itself with foolish tenderness.

> [1] *mixing with disreputable company*

Just as the king – then Henry Bolingbroke – had challenged and deposed King Richard, so he in turn is now threatened by Hotspur. But Henry is full of respect for the young man, with his ambition and his military prowess:

> King: … even as I was then is Percy now.
> Now by my sceptre, and my soul to boot,
> He hath more worthy interest[1] to the state
> Than thou the shadow of succession.[2]

> [1] *a more valid claim*
> [2] *the insubstantial custom of inheritance*

The king describes Hotspur's achievements with admiration. Despite his youth – he is no older than the prince – he has led armies of battle-hardened troops, and defeated the formidable Douglas more than once. Now, in alliance with Douglas, Mortimer and others, he is threatening the kingdom itself. Perhaps the prince will take his side, suggests the king:

> *King:*   Why, Harry, do I tell thee of my foes,
> Which art my nearest and dearest enemy?
> Thou that art like enough, through vassal[1] fear,
> Base inclination, and the start of spleen,[2]
> To fight against me under Percy's pay …

[1] *lowly*
[2] *impetuous bad temper*

This suggestion of cowardice and treason provokes an impassioned denial from Hal. He vows fervently to redeem his shameful past by confronting Hotspur in battle and defeating him utterly.

The king is pleased with his son's eagerness to fight, and he assures the prince that he will have a significant part to play in the forthcoming campaign against the rebels.

Sir Walter Blunt comes in with urgent news: a rebel army, of both English and Scottish troops, is gathering at Shrewsbury. The king remains calm. He is well informed of the activities of the rebels, and his forces are already on their way to confront them. Soon he and his son will be joining them.

News reaches the tavern

In the Boar's Head tavern, Falstaff is feeling sorry for himself. He is convinced he is losing weight and becoming ill. He talks briefly of repentance and changing his ways, but his heart is not in it. He teases Bardolph about his inflamed, reddened complexion:

> *Falstaff:*   Do thou amend thy face, and I'll amend my life …
> *Bardolph:*   Why, Sir John, my face does you no harm.
> *Falstaff:*   No, I'll be sworn, I make as good use of it as many
>   a man doth of a death's-head,[1] or a *memento mori*.
>   I never see thy face but I think[2] upon hell-fire …

> [1] *representation of a skull, typically set in a ring;*
>   *a reminder of mortality*
> [2] *without thinking*

When the hostess comes in, Falstaff asks her if she has discovered who picked his pocket during the night. She is offended at the thought that she allows thieves in her tavern, and reminds Falstaff of all the money that he owes her.

Hal enters in high spirits, bringing news of the coming war. But Falstaff and the hostess have other matters to discuss. Both try to gain Hal's attention, Falstaff over his stolen valuables and the hostess over Falstaff's slanders. The prince reveals that he knows the contents of Falstaff's pockets; there were no valuables, he points out, just bills from taverns and brothels. Falstaff pleads the proverbial frailty of the flesh:

> *Falstaff:*   Thou knowest in the state of innocency Adam fell,
>   and what should poor Jack Falstaff do in the days of
>   villainy? Thou seest I have more flesh than another
>   man, and therefore more frailty.

Hal mentions – to Falstaff's disapproval – that the money robbed from the travellers has been paid back. He also announces that, after this morning's discussion, he is now on good terms with his father. Falstaff and Bardolph are delighted; the prince will surely have access to unlimited funds now.

But the immediate concern is war. Falstaff learns that Hal has put him in charge of a company of foot-soldiers; he is dismayed at the idea of travelling on foot, but is sure he will be able to profit from the war one way or another.

The prince orders Falstaff to come to the rallying-point tomorrow afternoon. He sends Bardolph off with letters to be delivered, while Peto is to ride off with Hal immediately on important business. With a final rousing speech, the prince sets off.

> *Prince:*   The land is burning, Percy stands on high,
>   And either we or they must lower lie.

Falstaff, pleased with developments but unwilling to leave the tavern, calls out for his breakfast.

"Once upon a time we were all Falstaffs ... there are some in whom the nostalgia for the state of innocent self-importance is so strong that they refuse to accept adult life and responsibilities and seek some means to become again the Falstaffs they once were. The commonest technique adopted is the bottle ..."

W. H. Auden, *The Prince's Dog*, 1959

The balance of power shifts

At the rebel camp in Shrewsbury, Hotspur is talking to his ally, the Scottish leader Douglas. The two men are expressing their respect for one another when a messenger arrives with a letter from Hotspur's father, the Earl of Northumberland.

The news is bad; Northumberland is gravely ill. He has been confined to his bed for four days, and cannot lead his army to Shrewsbury. There is no one else he can trust to take command of his troops at short notice. Nevertheless, he encourages Hotspur to press on with the rebellion, particularly as the king is by now well aware of the rebels' intentions.

Northumberland's absence is a severe setback. Hotspur and Douglas, however, quickly take a positive view of the situation: rather than risking everything in one battle, they can fight the enemy all the more vigorously in their current state, knowing that reinforcements, in the form of Northumberland's army, will be available at a later date.

Worcester, Northumberland's brother, takes a less optimistic view. His brother's absence may result in rumours, questioning and doubt amongst their supporters at a time when unity is essential. Hotspur disagrees:

> *Hotspur:*   I rather of his absence make this use:
> It lends a lustre and more great opinion,
> A larger dare to our great enterprise,
> Than if the Earl were here; for men must think
> If we without his help can make a head[1]
> To push against a kingdom, with his help
> We shall o'erturn it topsy-turvy down.

[1] *raise a fighting force; advance*

Another messenger, Sir Richard Vernon, now arrives at the camp. He reports that the response to the rebellion is under way. The Earl of Westmoreland is heading towards the rebel camp, in command of seven thousand troops; and the king himself is about to join the march towards Shrewsbury.

Hotspur is untroubled by the news. He enquires what the king's son and his associates, notorious for their unruliness, are doing. Vernon replies that he has seen the prince and his troops with his own eyes. They were an impressive sight:

> *Vernon:*   All furnish'd, all in arms;
> All plum'd like estridges[1] ...
> Glittering in golden coats like images,[2]
> As full of spirit as the month of May,
> And gorgeous as the sun at midsummer;
> Wanton[3] as youthful goats, wild as young bulls.

> [1] *wearing ostrich feathers (the emblem of the Prince of Wales)*
> [2] *gilded statues of warriors*
> [3] *lively, exuberant*

Vernon's admiring description of the prince irritates Hotspur, and he vows to face the Prince of Wales in single combat. Impatient for battle, he is eager for Glendower to join them.

At this point Vernon breaks yet more unwelcome news: it will be at least a fortnight before Glendower's army is assembled. Douglas and Worcester are both stunned. It is clear that the rebels will be greatly outnumbered by the king's forces. The rebellion must go ahead, Hotspur declares recklessly.

On the march

Falstaff is making his way, with his troop of infantry, towards Shrewsbury. He orders Bardolph, one of his company, to go and buy him a bottle of sack. Bardolph grumbles at having to buy the wine, yet again, out of his own money.

When Bardolph is gone, Falstaff reflects guiltily on the company of soldiers he has assembled. Hal, as promised, has made him a captain, and he has the right to conscript men into his company of foot-soldiers whether they are willing or not. He has used his power to enlist those who are both reluctant to fight and rich enough to pay him for exemption from military service.

> *Falstaff:* I press me none but good householders, yeomen's sons, inquire me out contracted bachelors[1] ... such as fear the report of a caliver[2] worse than a struck fowl or a hurt wild duck.

[1] *men who are engaged to be married*
[2] *the bang of a light gun*

"*For most of Shakespeare's adult life, England had been struggling to resist Spanish expansionism, fuelled by the plunder of the New World. The Queen's interest in the booty that could be seized from Spanish galleons was not simply greed but necessity. A series of Continental wars had so depleted the English exchequer that she was forced to resort to various kinds of unpopular emergency taxation, while the common people lived in continual fear of impressment for active service. Shakespeare's portrait of Falstaff as a corrupt recruiting officer has always been appreciated as comic; its implications go far deeper ... Corruption of those in public life was certainly widespread in England in the 1590s; it seems possible that Falstaff excited not only laughter but jeering and cat-calls.*"

Germaine Greer, *Shakespeare*, 1986

Having taken the wealthier men's money, Falstaff has replaced them with an assortment of impoverished down-and-outs and petty criminals:

> *Falstaff:* ... such as indeed were never soldiers, but discarded unjust serving-men,[1] younger sons to younger brothers, revolted[2] tapsters, and ostlers trade-fallen,[3] the cankers[4] of a calm world and a long peace ... No eye hath seen such scarecrows.

[1] *servants dismissed for dishonesty*
[2] *runaway*
[3] *stable-hands who have lost their jobs*
[4] *unhealthy products*

... the cankers of a calm world and a long peace

This negative view of long periods of peace was widely held at the time. For many, the ideal was to engage in triumphant wars abroad, while maintaining peace and order at home:

"No body can be healthful without exercise, neither natural body nor politic; and certainly, to a kingdom or estate, a just and honourable war is the true exercise. A civil war, indeed, is like the heat of a fever; but a foreign war is like the heat of exercise, and serveth to keep the body in health; for in a slothful peace, both courages will effeminate and manners will corrupt."

Francis Bacon, *Of the True Greatness of Kingdoms and Estates*, 1612

Falstaff unexpectedly meets Hal and the Earl of Westmoreland, who are hastening towards Shrewsbury. Both men comment on the ragged state of his company. They are good enough for their purpose, replies Falstaff cynically.

> *Prince:*   I did never see such pitiful rascals.
> *Falstaff:*   Tut, tut, good enough to toss,[1] food for powder[2] ...
> *Westmoreland:* Ay, but, Sir John, methinks they are exceeding
> poor and bare,[3] too beggarly.
> *Falstaff:*   Faith, for their poverty I know not where they had
> that; and for their bareness I am sure they never
> learned that of me.
>
> [1] *to be impaled on a pike or spear*
> [2] *cannon-fodder*
> [3] *lean, skinny*

Hal and Westmoreland go quickly on their way. Falstaff, not wishing to arrive at the battle until it is nearly over, proceeds at an unhurried pace.

Hotspur airs his grievances   IV, iii

In the rebel camp, Hotspur and Douglas are arguing for an immediate attack on the king's forces. Vernon and Worcester are vehemently opposed to the idea: they should wait for the expected reinforcements, and in any case many of their cavalry have not had time to rest, and are weary after their long journey.

The argument is interrupted by a trumpet-call. Sir Walter Blunt, the king's adviser, has come to negotiate with the rebels.

Hotspur welcomes him, expressing regret that he has not joined their cause. Sir Walter replies coldly that he will never be disloyal to the anointed king. He makes a formal statement of the king's offer: if the rebels have in any way been mistreated by the king – who greatly appreciates the service done for him by the Percy family – he wishes them to state their grievances.

The king promises not only to satisfy them, Sir Walter explains, but to pardon the leaders of the rebellion and their allies.

> Blunt: ... He bids you name your griefs, and with all speed
> You shall have your desires with interest
> And pardon absolute for yourself, and these
> Herein misled by your suggestion.[1]

> [1] *instigation, incitement*

Hotspur maintains a superficially courteous manner, but is sceptical of the offer. King Henry always acts in his own interests:

> Hotspur: The King is kind, and well we know the King
> Knows at what time to promise, when to pay ...

He goes on to recount how his family helped Henry when, as a young man, he returned from exile to claim the title of Duke of Lancaster and the lands that were rightfully his. The young man became ever more ambitious, abusing his power and whipping up popular support. When King Richard was engaged in the war in Ireland, Henry had the king's trusted deputies executed. Finally he deposed the rightful king and, claims Hotspur, had him murdered.

When Hotspur's brother-in-law Mortimer, who had a better claim to the throne, was captured in Wales, Henry refused to pay his ransom to free him. Hotspur himself, who fought against the Scots invaders on the king's behalf, has been slighted by the king; similarly, his father and uncle have both been treated disrespectfully. It is hardly surprising, concludes Hotspur, that they have united against the king in an act of self-defence. Besides, the king's entitlement to the throne is questionable; his reign can surely not last long.

Sir Walter asks Hotspur what reply he should take to the king. Setting aside his sense of anger and injustice, Hotspur tells him, calmly, to inform the king that they will consider his offer. His uncle Worcester will come to the king in the morning to tell him of their intentions.

Urging Hotspur to accept the king's offer of pardon, Sir Walter leaves the rebel camp.

The medieval period, in which the events of *Henry IV* take place, held an intense fascination for the Victorians. It had a profound influence on their art and architecture, epitomised in London's Houses of Parliament, designed and built in the mid-19th century.

Against this background, Shakespeare's history plays were often viewed as colourful pageants of kings, courtiers and knights in armour. Hotspur in particular was seen, despite his faults, as a model of the medieval virtues of courage and chivalry. As the century drew to a close, a more sceptical, less romantic view emerged:

"Hotspur does not scruple, for the sake of avenging private wrongs, to enter into a league with his country's hereditary foes. He consents to see England broken up, and claims a third share of the booty ... Shakespeare laid bare the fatal flaw of the medieval system – its glorification of individual 'honour' and prowess at the expense of national well-being."

F. S. Boas, *Shakespeare and His Predecessors*, 1896

A sense of foreboding

The Archbishop of York, a supporter of the rebels, is dispatching urgent messages from his palace to other trusted allies. He is pessimistic about the outcome of tomorrow's battle. Without the armies of Northumberland, Mortimer, or Glendower – whose powers of prophecy, he believes, have warned him to stay away from the battle – Hotspur is likely to be defeated by the king's superior forces.

The king is aware that there are other rebels such as himself, and will not hesitate to crush them:

> *Archbishop:* ... if Lord Percy thrive not, ere the King
> Dismiss his power[1] he means to visit us,
> For he hath heard of our confederacy,[2]
> And 'tis but wisdom to make strong against him ...
>
> [1] *army*
> [2] *alliance*

It is essential for the remaining rebels to be prepared.

In 1951, the year of the Festival of Britain, the four plays dealing with the rise and fall of Henry Bolingbroke and the accession of his son, Prince Hal – played by the 25-year-old Richard Burton – were staged together at Stratford-on-Avon: *Richard II*, *Henry IV Part 1*, *Henry IV Part 2*, and *Henry V*. At that time, the idea of presenting the four works as a sequence was ground-breaking, and many people started to see the plays in a new light.

One famous critic remembered the landmark season when reviewing a later production of *Henry IV*:

"I suspected it at Stratford four years ago, and now I am sure. For me the two parts of Henry IV *are the twin summits of Shakespeare's achievement ... great public plays in which a whole nation is under scrutiny and on trial."*

Kenneth Tynan, review in *The Observer*, 1955

The final offer

The king's army has set up camp near Shrewsbury. The sun is blood red in the early morning sky, and a blustery wind suggests that it will be a stormy day.

A trumpet sounds, and the Earl of Worcester, the rebels' envoy, enters the camp, accompanied by Sir Richard Vernon. The king immediately reproaches Worcester for the discord and conflict that he has brought about in the kingdom. Worcester replies that, for his part, he would prefer a quiet life; the current conflict is not of his making.

When the king asks him to explain himself, Worcester sets out – just as Hotspur had done earlier – the Percy family's sense of grievance. They had supported the young Henry Bolingbroke in his quest to obtain his rightful inheritance on the death of his father, John of Gaunt, whose lands and wealth had been confiscated by King Richard. Worcester reminds the king of the promise he made at the time:

> *Worcester:*   You swore to us,
> And you did swear that oath at Doncaster,
> That you did nothing purpose 'gainst the state,[1]
> Nor claim no further than your new-fall'n right,
> The seat[2] of Gaunt, dukedom of Lancaster.
> To this we swore our aid …

[1] *you had no designs on the kingdom*
[2] *lands, estate*

But as Henry grew in ambition, he broke his vow, made a bid for power, took the crown, and rejected those who had helped him. Worcester insists that the king's actions have forced the Percys, for their own safety, to take the defensive position in which they now find themselves.

King Henry does not respond directly to Worcester's claims. The Percys' real motive is not defence but rebellion pure and simple, he says, accusing them of using flimsy arguments to win the support of the needy and the dissatisfied, who are always attracted by disorder and anarchy.

> *King:*   These things indeed you have articulate,
>   Proclaim'd at market crosses, read in churches,
>   To face the garment of rebellion
>   With some fine colour that may please the eye
>   Of fickle changelings and poor discontents …

… fickle changelings and poor discontents

London in Shakespeare's time was an overcrowded and often disorderly city. There were several serious outbreaks of rioting in the 1590s, and the authorities were nervous of any gatherings that could lead to criminal or political disturbances. They were particularly concerned about the many theatres that had sprung up in recent years, most of which were located in areas outside their jurisdiction.

The city authorities, dominated by religious Puritans, frequently appealed to those in power to regulate the theatres more strictly, or to close them down altogether. This letter from London's Lord Mayor to the Queen's Privy Council in 1597 is typical:

"We have signified to your Honours many times heretofore the great inconvenience which we find to grow by the common exercise of stage-plays … being of that frame and matter as usually they are, containing nothing but profane fables, lascivious matters, cozening devices,[1] and scurrilous behaviours … they give opportunity to the evil-disposed and ungodly people that are within and about this city to assemble themselves and to make their matches[2] for all their lewd and ungodly practices …"

[1] *plots involving trickery and deception*
[2] *assignations, rendezvous*

However, theatre companies such as Shakespeare's benefited from the patronage of influential figures in the Queen's court, and could usually withstand the authorities' disapproval.

The prince now makes a proposal. First he tells Worcester that he has enormous respect for his nephew Hotspur, who – setting aside his involvement in the present rebellion – is rightly regarded as the noblest and most courageous young gentleman of his time. The prince admits that his own reputation, as Hotspur himself has alleged, is very different.

> Prince: For my part, I may speak it to my shame,
> I have a truant been to chivalry,
> And so I hear he doth account me too ...

If the two armies meet in battle, many lives will be lost on both sides; instead, he, the heir to the throne, is ready to face Hotspur in single combat.

The king is not against the idea in principle, he says, but it is not the solution to the crisis. The rebels must lay down their arms, in return for a general amnesty for all involved.

> King: ... no, good Worcester, no,
> We love our people well, even those we love
> That are misled upon your cousin's part,[1]
> And will they[2] take the offer of our grace[3]
> Both he, and they, and you, yea, every man
> Shall be my friend again, and I'll be his ...

> [1] *we even love those who have taken the*
> *wrong path in supporting Hotspur*
> [2] *if they will*
> [3] *mercy, pardon*

Failure to agree will result in terrible punishment and eventual defeat. This is the message that must be taken back, says the king, urging them to consider his offer carefully. With this he gives Worcester leave to return to the rebel camp.

Falstaff reaches a conclusion

Once Worcester has gone, Hal remarks that the offer will surely be rejected; Douglas and Hotspur together have the confidence to take on the world. The king orders his commanders to be prepared for battle.

As the preparations begin in earnest, Falstaff takes the prince aside and asks him to come to his rescue if he needs help during the fighting. He will have to look after himself, replies Hal. Besides, like everyone else, he has to die sooner or later; the best thing to do is pray.

On his own, Falstaff reflects that he does not wish to invite death before it is due. He wants to keep out of harm's way. It is only the desire for honour that might spur him on into danger; but what if the same honour has him marked down as a casualty? And what is honour, in reality? He mulls over the word, determined to tease out its meaning.

Falstaff: Can honour set to[1] a leg? No. Or an arm? No. Or take away the grief of a wound? No. Honour hath no skill in surgery then? No. What is honour? A word. What is in that word honour? What is that honour? Air. … Who hath it? He that died a-Wednesday. Doth he feel it? No. Doth he hear it? No. 'Tis insensible,[2] then? Yea, to the dead. But will it not live with the living? No. Why? Detraction will not suffer it.[3]

[1] *set, repair*
[2] *impossible to perceive with the senses*
[3] *slander and gossip will not allow it to live*

Honour, as far as Falstaff is concerned, is not worth possessing – and certainly not worth dying for.

Falstaff: Therefore I'll none of it. Honour is a mere scutcheon[1] – and so ends my catechism.

[1] *a coat of arms painted on wood or canvas, hung in a church to commemorate a dead nobleman*

To audiences of the Restoration period, some fifty years after Shakespeare's death, his plays, while still admired, sometimes seemed sprawling and unrefined. Playwrights often adapted them freely to suit current tastes, while some – including many of the history plays – were neglected altogether. *Henry IV, Part 1*, however, remained popular throughout the period. No doubt this was due, at least in part, to the presence of Falstaff.

One famous visitor to the fashionable Drury Lane Theatre, though not particularly impressed by the play in general, was very taken with William Cartwright's performance as the fat knight. Apart from that, it was the audience rather than the play that engaged his attention:

"To the King's playhouse and there saw 'Henry the Fourth'; and contrary to expectation, was pleased in nothing more than in Cartwright's speaking of Falstaff's speech about 'What is honour?' The house full of Parliament-men, it being holiday with them; and it was observable how a gentleman of good habit, sitting just before us, eating of some fruit in the midst of the play, did drop down as dead, being choked; but with much ado Orange Moll did thrust her fingers down his throat, and brought him to life again."

Samuel Pepys, diary entry for 2nd November 1667

A calculated lie

Back in the rebel camp, Worcester is discussing the king's offer with Vernon. Worcester is adamant that the offer of amnesty must not be made known to Hotspur. He is convinced that, even if they are all pardoned as promised, the king will never forget their rebellion, and will eventually find a pretext for taking his revenge.

> *Worcester:* O no, my nephew must not know, Sir Richard,
> The liberal and kind offer of the King.
> *Vernon:* 'Twere best he did.
> *Worcester:*   Then are we all undone.[1]
> It is not possible, it cannot be,
> The King should keep his word in loving us;
> He will suspect us still,[2] and find a time
> To punish this offence in other faults ...

> [1] *we would be destroyed*
> [2] *constantly*

The Percy family will never be trusted again and, in turn, they will never be able to trust others. Even if they are treated well they will need to be on their guard:

> *Worcester:* ... we shall feed like oxen at a stall,
> The better cherish'd still the nearer death.[1]

> [1] *who are fed best when they are being prepared*
> *for slaughter*

While the impetuous young Hotspur may be forgiven in time, the older generation of Worcester and Northumberland will never shake off the accusation of treachery, and are likely to pay with their lives. It is imperative that the king's offer is rejected. Vernon is doubtful, but agrees to go along with Worcester's deception.

When Hotspur and Douglas enter and ask about his negotiations with the king, Worcester accordingly tells them that the king is determined to fight.

Worcester: There is no seeming mercy[1] in the King.
Hotspur: Did you beg any? God forbid!
Worcester: I told him gently of our grievances …

> [1] *nothing resembling mercy*

The Earl of Westmoreland, the king's ally who has been held at the rebel camp as surety during the negotiations, is sent back to the king's camp with a message of defiance. War is now inevitable.

Worcester mentions Hal's offer of single combat. Hotspur relishes the idea, and asks whether the prince made his challenge in a spirit of contempt. Quite the opposite, replies Vernon; he was modest and respectful.

Vernon speaks warmly of the prince, who demonstrated both honesty about his own shortcomings and generosity in praise of his opponent. Hotspur is unimpressed:

Vernon: … let me tell the world –
          If he outlive the envy[1] of this day,
          England did never owe[2] so sweet a hope
          So much misconstru'd in his wantonness.[3]
Hotspur: Cousin, I think thou art enamoured
          On his follies: never did I hear
          Of any prince so wild a liberty.[4]

> [1] *hostility, aggression*
> [2] *possess*
> [3] *so wrongly considered to be degenerate*
> [4] *such irresponsible, reckless freedom*

Hotspur intends to meet the prince on the field of battle. Whatever his virtues may be, Hotspur intends to prevail. He calls to his troops to arm themselves and lift their spirits. A messenger comes into the camp with letters, but Hotspur ignores him; time is short, and they have urgent business in hand.

Hotspur: ... if we live, we live to tread on[1] kings,
                If die, brave death when princes die with us!

> [1] *crush, defeat*

Another messenger rushes in; the king has launched his attack. As the trumpets sound in the rebel camp, Hotspur calls for his troops to bid one another farewell.

Hotspur: Sound all the lofty instruments of war,
            And by that music let us all embrace,
            For, heaven to earth,[1] some of us never shall
            A second time do such a courtesy.

> [1] *the odds are as great as heaven is to earth*

The rebels charge out into the field, and battle commences.

The battle of Shrewsbury was fought, after lengthy negotiations had failed, on the afternoon of 21st July 1403. Exact numbers are not known, but the battle probably involved about thirty thousand troops. Both sides used longbows to deadly effect. As a chronicler of the time records, the rebels discharged the first shower of arrows:

"Therefore the archers of Henry Percy began the fight ... men fell on the king's side as fast as leaves fall in autumn after the hoar-frost."

By the end of the day, some five thousand men were dead or severely wounded. The Prince of Wales, sixteen years old at the time, was struck by an arrow in the face: it could not be removed for several days, and left the future king with a permanent scar.

Mistaken identity

As the fighting rages, the Scottish leader Douglas is trying to track down King Henry. Coming across a nobleman in the king's colours, he believes he has found him; and the man confirms that he is indeed king. Douglas demands his surrender, warning him that he has already taken the life of one man claiming to be the king. The nobleman refuses to yield, and Douglas kills him in the ensuing struggle.

Hotspur comes upon the scene and recognises the body. It is not the king, he tells Douglas, but Sir Walter Blunt, a gallant and trusted knight. Many in the royal army are disguised as the king, he explains. Douglas vows to slaughter them, one by one, until he finds the true king. The battle is going well for the rebels, Hotspur declares, and he and Douglas enter the fray once more.

Falstaff is out of place

Falstaff is doing his best to keep away from the heat of the action. The violent battlefield is nothing like his usual surroundings:

Falstaff: Though I could scape shot-free[1] at London, I fear
the shot here, here's no scoring[2] but upon the pate.[3]

[1] *scot-free; without paying the bill*
[2] *adding items to an account instead of paying*
     immediately; alternatively, cutting or wounding
[3] *head*

He comes across Blunt's body. He has no doubt died honourably, reflects Falstaff, but he has no wish to join the nobleman. Most of his ragged collection of foot-soldiers are dead or wounded:

Falstaff: I have led my ragamuffins where they are peppered;[1]
there's not three of my hundred and fifty left alive,
and they are for the town's end, to beg during life.

[1] *riddled with wounds*

The prince stumbles upon Falstaff, and demands to know why he is away from the action. Falstaff replies that he is catching his breath after a ferocious bout of combat; in fact, he has slain Hotspur himself.

Hal scoffs at his foolish stories, knowing that Hotspur is still alive. He tells Falstaff to lend him his sword, but the old man is reluctant to part with it. Instead, he offers his pistol, warning him that it has been used heavily and is still hot.

The prince hastily grabs Falstaff's pistol-case and opens it; but it contains no weapon, just a bottle of sack. Hal throws the bottle at him, furious that he should be joking at a time like this, and sets off back into the field.

On his own, Falstaff takes another uneasy look at the corpse of Sir Walter Blunt. He will keep out of Hotspur's way, Falstaff tells himself; if he dies an honourable death, it will not be out of choice.

> *Falstaff:* I like not such grinning honour as Sir Walter hath. Give me life, which if I can save, so: if not, honour comes unlooked for, and there's an end.

The prince confronts his adversaries V, iv

King Henry has withdrawn briefly from the battlefield. He sees that Hal is wounded, and asks his younger son, John of Lancaster, to take him to safety.

John is unwilling to stay away from the fighting any longer than necessary, and soon returns to the field. The prince too, despite his wounds, decides to return to the conflict, inspired by his younger brother's example. Besides, the rebels have the upper hand:

> *Prince:* … God forbid a shallow scratch should drive
> The Prince of Wales from such a field as this,
> Where stain'd nobility lies trodden on,
> And rebels' arms triumph in massacres!

Douglas, searching the battlefield for the king, now encounters Henry, who is at present on his own. Unsure whether he is the genuine king or in disguise, Douglas challenges him, and the two men fight.

Douglas is a fearsome fighter, and the king is soon in difficulty; however, the prince now returns. He confronts Douglas, vowing to take retribution for the noblemen that the Scot has slaughtered. The prince gains the upper hand, and Douglas retreats. Hal is eager to return to the action, but the king asks him to pause.

King: Stay and breathe a while:
       Thou hast redeem'd thy lost opinion,[1]
       And show'd thou mak'st some tender of[2] my life,
       In this fair rescue thou hast brought to me.
Prince: O God, they did me too much injury
       That ever said I hearken'd for[3] your death.

[1] *your bad reputation*
[2] *have some regard for*
[3] *was looking forward to*

The king returns to the battle. Hal is about to do the same when Hotspur arrives. The two young men challenge one another:

Prince: ... think not, Percy,
       To share with me in glory any more:
       Two stars keep not their motion in one sphere,[1]
       Nor can one England brook[2] a double reign
       Of Harry Percy and the Prince of Wales.
Hotspur: Nor shall it, Harry, for the hour is come
       To end the one of us ...

[1] *cannot occupy the same orbit*
[2] *tolerate*

As the two men fight, Falstaff approaches, and watches excitedly from a safe distance. But to his terror, Douglas returns, and is about to attack him. Falstaff immediately feigns death.

In the meantime, the prince has mortally wounded Hotspur. The hurt to his pride is worse than the hurt to his body, says Hotspur, dying; but thoughts of his lost honour, like his life itself, must come to an end.

> *Hotspur:*   But thoughts, the slaves of life, and life, time's fool,
> And time, that takes survey of all the world,
> Must have a stop.

Hal treats his rival's body with great respect, covering Hotspur's face with an ornament from his own armour. He contemplates the sad sight of greatness led astray by ill-conceived ambition.

> *Prince:*   When that this body did contain a spirit,
> A kingdom for it was too small a bound;[1]
> But now two paces of the vilest earth
> Is room enough. This earth that bears thee dead
> Bears not alive so stout[2] a gentleman.
> ... Thy ignominy sleep with thee in the grave,
> But not remember'd in thy epitaph!

[1] *boundary*
[2] *valiant*

Falstaff comes back to life

As he leaves, the prince sees Falstaff's motionless body on the ground. He is sorry at the death of his friend, but he knows that his own life has changed profoundly. He remains philosophical, and amused as ever at the old man's bulk.

> *Prince:*   What, old acquaintance, could not all this flesh
> Keep in a little life? Poor Jack, farewell!
> ... O, I should have a heavy miss[1] of thee
> If I were much in love with vanity:[2]
> Death hath not struck so fat a deer today ...

[1] *I would feel a heavy loss*
[2] *frivolity, triviality*

When the prince has gone, Falstaff raises himself from the ground. He had to counterfeit death, he tells himself, or else the bloodthirsty Douglas would have killed him. But there is no dishonesty in what he did, he reasons:

> *Falstaff:*   ... I am no counterfeit: to die is to be a counterfeit, for he is but the counterfeit of a man, who hath not the life of a man: but to counterfeit dying, when a man thereby liveth, is to be no counterfeit, but the true and perfect image of life indeed. The better part of valour is discretion,[1] in the which better part I have saved my life.

> [1] *judgement, good sense*

Falstaff considers Hotspur's lifeless body, lying nearby. Perhaps he too is faking death, it occurs to him; and if Hotspur were to come back to life, he would easily overpower Falstaff. With a quick look around to make sure that no one is watching, Falstaff takes out his sword and stabs Hotspur in the thigh. Confident that the young man is dead, Falstaff picks up his body and carries it away: he intends to claim the honour of having killed the rebel leader.

The better part of valour is discretion ...

This was a well-known saying of the time, meaning that courage should be tempered with wisdom; without discretion, valour may descend into the wild foolhardiness typified by Hotspur.

Falstaff conveniently misinterprets the phrase, taking it to mean that consideration of his own safety should override any notions of courageous action. Interestingly, it is Falstaff's interpretation that is now generally assumed to be the proverb's true meaning.

High hopes

The prince and his younger brother John of Lancaster now pass by. Hal is amazed to see his old friend alive. Falstaff confirms that he is not dead, and proudly lays Hotspur's body on the ground in front of them:

> *Falstaff:* If your father will do me any honour, so: if not, let him kill the next Percy himself. I look to be either earl or duke, I can assure you.

Hal points out that he killed Hotspur himself. On the contrary, explains Falstaff, Hotspur, like Falstaff himself, was not dead after his clash with the prince, just out of breath. When Hotspur recovered, there had been a long, hard fight between the two men, ending in Hotspur's death. As evidence, he points out the wound on Hotspur's thigh.

Hal's brother is amazed at Falstaff's account. Hal, used to the old man's fraudulent claims, agrees good-humouredly to back up his unlikely story if it will benefit him.

> *John:* This is the strangest tale that ever I heard.
> *Prince:* This is the strangest fellow, brother John …
> [*to Falstaff*] For my part, if a lie may do thee grace,
> I'll gild[1] it with the happiest[2] terms I have.

> [1] *decorate, embellish*
> [2] *most positive*

A trumpet sounds from the battlefield: the rebel army is in retreat. The battle is over. The prince and his brother make their way towards a vantage-point from which they can survey the field. Falstaff, still lugging Hotspur's corpse with him, follows on behind.

Confident that he will be generously rewarded for killing Hotspur, Falstaff is already making plans for his new life as an aristocrat. There will be no more depravity, drinking, or gluttony:

Falstaff: He that rewards me, God reward him! If I do grow great, I'll grow less,[1] for I'll purge,[2] and leave[3] sack, and live cleanly as a nobleman should do.

[1] *thinner*
[2] *repent*
[3] *give up*

"... by the play's end, Hal casts an inclusive shadow. He has met the claims of Hotspur's world, of Falstaff's, and of Henry's, without narrowing himself to any one. He has practiced mercy as well as justice, politics as well as friendship, shown himself capable of mockery as well as reverence, detachment as well as commitment, and brought into a practicable balance court, field, and tavern. He is on the way to becoming the luminous figure toward whom, in Henry V, *Welshman, Irishman, Scot, and Englishman will alike be drawn. In this figure, combining valor, courtliness, hard sense, and humor in an ideal image of the potentialities of the English character, Shakespeare seems to have discerned grounds for that optimism about the future of his country which permeates his historical vision ..."*

Maynard Mack, Introduction to the Signet Classic edition of *Henry IV, Part 1*, 1986

Unfinished business

King Henry has brought his sons and noblemen together on the battlefield. Although his troops have defeated the rebels, the king's mood is far from triumphant. When the captured Earl of Worcester is brought before him, the king addresses him in anger and sorrow, having discovered that his offer of amnesty was not passed on to the rebel leaders.

> *King:* Ill-spirited Worcester, did not we send grace,
> Pardon, and terms of love to all of you?
> And wouldst thou turn our offers contrary?

Many precious lives have been lost today that might have been saved if his offer had been passed on and considered, says the king. Worcester replies that he was motivated by his desire for security; but he is now resigned to his fate. The king sends him away for execution, along with his co-conspirator Sir Richard Vernon.

The prince reports that Douglas has been caught. Having heard of Hotspur's death, and seeing his own men deserting in panic, the leader of the Scots had fled himself and, stumbling, was captured and brought to the prince's tent.

Hal asks to be allowed to deal with Douglas himself, and the king consents. However, the prince, far from ordering his death, tells his brother to release the Scotsman, who – unlike the treasonous Worcester – is a valiant and respected foe.

> *Prince:* … Go to the Douglas and deliver him
> Up to his pleasure, ransomless and free:
> His valours shown upon our crests[1] today
> Have taught us how to cherish such high deeds,
> Even in the bosom of our adversaries.

> [1] *shown by the damage done to our helmets*

The task of overcoming rebellion is not yet over, the king announces. The army is to be split into two divisions. One, under the command of his younger son John and the trusted Earl of Westmoreland, will march on York, where they will face the combined troops of the Archbishop and the Earl of Northumberland, Hotspur's father. The second, headed by the king and prince Harry, is to tackle Glendower and the challenger Mortimer in Wales.

If the spirit of today's success can be maintained, the nation will once more be united under King Henry:

> King: Rebellion in this land shall lose his sway,[1]
> Meeting the check of such another day,[2]
> And since this business so fair is done,
> Let us not leave till all our own be won.
>
> [1] *power, influence*
> [2] *meeting resistance such as we have shown today*

The remaining rebels are arming themselves in readiness for war, and there is no time to lose. Soon the field is empty as the king, his sons, his commanders and his soldiers all depart: there are further battles to be fought.

———
———

Acknowledgements

The following publications have proved invaluable as sources of factual information and critical insight:

- Jonathan Bate, *Soul of the Age*, Penguin Books, 2008

- Charles Boyce, *Shakespeare A to Z*, Roundtable Press, 1990

- Terry Eagleton, *William Shakespeare*, Blackwell, 1986

- Nicholas Fogg, *Hidden Shakespeare*, Amberley Publishing, 2012

- Levi Fox, *The Shakespeare Handbook*, Bodley Head, 1987

- Northrop Frye, *On Shakespeare*, Yale University Press, 1986

- Germaine Greer, *Shakespeare*, in the *Past Masters* series, Oxford University Press, 1986

- David Hilliam, *Kings, Queens, Bones and Bastards*, Sutton Publishing, 1998

- A. R. Humphreys, Introduction to the Arden edition of *Henry IV, Part 1*, Methuen, 1960

- Ronald Knowles, *Henry IV Parts 1 and 2*, in *The Critics Debate* series, Macmillan, 1992

- Maynard Mack, Introduction to the Signet Classic edition of *Henry IV, Part 1*, NAL Penguin Inc., 1986

- John Wain, *The Living World of Shakespeare*, Pelican Books, 1964

- Stanley Wells (editor), *The Cambridge Companion to Shakespeare Studies*, Cambridge University Press, 1984

- John Dover Wilson, *Life in Shakespeare's England*, Pelican Books, 1944

All quotations from *Henry IV, Part 1* are taken from the Arden Shakespeare.

You can order the *Shakespeare Handbooks*
direct from the publisher.

Visit: **www.shakespeare-handbooks.com**

Call: **01323 811187**

Free postage & packing in the UK.
Overseas customers please allow £1 per book.

Titles currently available in the *Shakespeare Handbooks* series are:

❑ **Antony & Cleopatra** (ISBN 978 1 899747 02 3, £4.95)

❑ **As You Like It** (ISBN 978 1 899747 00 9, £4.95)

❑ **Hamlet** (ISBN 978 1 899747 07 8, £4.95)

❑ **Henry IV, Part 1** (ISBN 978 1 899747 05 4, £4.95)

❑ **King Lear** (ISBN 978 1 899747 03 0, £4.95)

❑ **Macbeth** (ISBN 978 1 899747 04 7, £4.95)

❑ **A Midsummer Night's Dream** (ISBN 978 1 899747 09 2, £4.95)

❑ **Romeo & Juliet** (ISBN 978 1 899747 10 8, £4.95)

❑ **Twelfth Night** (ISBN 978 1 899747 01 6, £4.95)

Upstart Crow Publications will not pass your address on to other organisations.

Prices correct at time of going to press. Whilst every effort is made to keep prices low, Upstart Crow Publications reserves the right to show new retail prices on covers which may differ from those previously advertised in the text or elsewhere.